MARGARET NEYLON
IT ALL ADDS UP

D1089645

Margaret Neylon has been involved in the holistic healing field for many years. Her first book, *Pathways*, was published by Attic Press in 1990. She has also written *Open Your Heart to Angel Love* (Angelgate Publishing, 1996) and *Angel Magic* (Thorsons, 2001). Margaret gives courses on numerology and related matters in venues all over Ireland. She lives in Virginia, County Cavan.

NEW ISLAND *Open Door*

IT ALL ADDS UP
First published January 2002
by New Island
2 Brookside
Dundrum Road
Dublin 14

www.newisland.ie

A CIP catalogue record for this book is available from the British Library

ISBN 1 902602 73 0

New Island Books receives financial assistance from
The Arts Council (An Chomhairle Ealaíon), Dublin, Ireland.

Typeset by New Island
Printed in Ireland by ColourBooks
Cover design by Artmark

1 3 5 4 2

Dear Reader,

On behalf of myself and the other contributing authors, I would like to welcome you to the third Open Door series. We hope that you enjoy the books and that reading becomes a lasting pleasure in your life.

Warmest wishes,

Patricia Scanlan.

Patricia Scanlan
Series Editor

To Patricia

For her support and friendship

Introduction

When I was at school I hated anything to do with figures. They never made sense to me. When I left home and started a job, I was just about able to cope with the basics of adding and taking away when it came to my pay cheque at the end of the week.

It's strange that I am now an expert on numbers, but not the kind we learnt at school. I grew interested in the science of numbers (which is called numerology) only a decade or so ago. Since then, working with numbers makes perfect sense to me. By knowing how to look into the future with the help of numerology, I have learned to succeed at a lot of things with not much effort.

The science of numbers is a broad subject. It can be used for just about anything in the world, and by anyone! I want to share some of what I know about numbers with you so that you, too, can bring about changes in your life. You see, the reason most of us don't succeed at things is not because we're stupid, it's just that we do things at the wrong time. It was the same for me. I wasn't stupid and I wasn't lazy. I just didn't know any better. Now I do, and life has become much simpler for me. Now I know when to start something and when to do nothing. I know when to have a first date and the best day to make up after an argument.

I know the best day to ask for a pay rise and when to hand in my notice!

The secret of numbers is quite simple. You don't have to be an expert in maths – I'm not. All you have to do is add two single numbers together and you've got the basics.

This science isn't just a 'new age' craze. It's very old. In fact some people believe it's as old as the Pyramids in Egypt. For many centuries, people all over the world have known about the power of numbers. Parents in Japan always count the number of brush-strokes in a child's name before choosing it for their baby! Some people won't even buy a house if the number isn't right for them. Most people would believe that they have a lucky number, so the 'secret' has been with us for some time.

There are many different areas of

our lives and many different numbers which affect each of those areas: love, family, ambition, career, money, home, health. That's what I want to talk about in this book.

The great thing about numerology is that it's as easy as adding 2 and 2 to make 4, or 1 and 6 to make 7. So if you want your life to become more simple and successful, read on!

1: Your Life Path Number

This is the number you were born with. It is like a code that you can refer to time and again as you go through your life. With it, you'll know if you're doing what you are meant to be doing. As it's based on the date of your birth, it's the most important number of all, for it can never change. Your Life Path Number tells you what you need to do in your life so that you can fulfil your destiny. The word 'destiny' is really the same as 'destination' or 'path'. When we're on the right path, we're sure to get to the right destination! The secret is to find out what that path is, and the first step is to find out your Life Path Number. The Life Path Numbers are numbers 1 to 11. What each number means is shown further on.

It's simple: just write down your full birth date and add up all the figures. Look at the following examples to see how it works. The chart below shows the months of the year and their numbers.

January	01
February	02
March	03
April	04
May	05
June	06
July	07
August	08
September	09
October	10
November	11
December	12

Example 1:

Amy was born on the 16th of December 1960. Write down the numbers of her birth date as below:

16   12   19   60

Now add them up, two digits at a time:

(Note, when two numbers add up to the number 10, it becomes a number 1, because 10 breaks down as a 1 and a 0: $1 + 0 = 1$.)

$$1+6 \quad 1+2 \quad 1+9 \quad 6+0$$
$$7 \; + \; 3 \quad\quad 1 \; + \; 6$$
$$1 \quad\quad + \quad\quad 7$$
$$8$$

So that final figure, 8, is Amy's Life Path Number.

Example 2:

Jack was born on the 24th of April 1943. Once again, set out the numbers as shown below, and add them up two digits at a time:

```
2+4   0+4   1+9   4+3
  6  +  4      1  +  7
      1      +    8
              9
```

So Jack's Life Path Number is 9.

Example 3:

Sarah was born on the 12th of March 1974. As we see below, her numbers require an extra piece of addition. This is because the last two digits in 1974 – that is, 7 and 4 – add up to 11. Because this is not a single number, we must add these two numbers together. $1 + 1 = 2$. So on the second line, the number 2 appears, rather than the number 11 (as you can see in the box below).

```
1+2   0+3   1+9   7+4
  3  +  3      1  + 2
      6      +    3
              9
```

Sarah's Life Path Number is 9.

Now work out your own Life Path Number following the method above. As you now know, that final digit is your Life Path Number. Remember to add up the full date, such as 1948, not just '48. Always write out the numbers in sets of 2 digits and add them up in a downward pattern as shown above, like an arrow pointing downward.

The best way to show your Life Path Number is to put it into a special symbol which is like the head of an arrow pointing down, for example:

This shows that you came down from heaven onto the earth. You brought with you a 'blueprint' or 'map' to follow which is set out in your Life

Path Number. Now all you have to do is find out what it is that you're meant to be doing by learning what each number means.

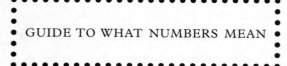

GUIDE TO WHAT NUMBERS MEAN

Number 1:

✓ *What you should do:*

Be unique. Be independent. Be innovative. Use your intelligence. Be ambitious.

Be the first person to do things. Be a natural leader. Have your own space. Be a decision maker.

✗ *What you should not do:*

Cut yourself off from others. Be co-dependent. Feel alone and lonely. Be eccentric. Be a loner and refuse to share with others.

Number 2:

✓ *What you should do:*

Have good relationships. Respond to other people's needs. Make your own choices. Take responsibility for your actions. Realise that it's not what happens that's important, it's how you react to what happens that brings about the result.

✗ *What you should not do:*

Be co-dependent. Blame others for what happens to you. Feel like a victim of life. Be unwilling to make decisions. Refuse to co-operate with others.

Number 3:

✓ *What you should do:*

Be creative. Be able to express yourself

through music, song, dance, painting, writing, cooking, gardening. Be able to show your emotions: cry and laugh, be joyful. Create your own world as a child does. Have a happy balance between your spiritual, mental and physical needs.

What you should not do:

Hold on to old hurts and pain. Refuse to express yourself and develop depression (which is the opposite of expression). Lack emotional expression. Be childish.

Number 4:

What you should do:

Empower yourself, which means find things out for yourself and don't be influenced by others. Be stable and work hard to make yourself secure. Be of great service to others. Have a certain amount of order in your life.

✖ *What you should not do:*

Be unstable and expect others to make you secure. Be a workaholic, slogging away like a slave and never getting anywhere. Use force, anger, or be a bully. Be imprisoned by fear. Live in chaos or be too regimented.

Number 5:

✓ *What you should do:*

Face conflict when it arises. Change when you need to change. Take a chance by doing something different. Break negative patterns. Make your own freedom, rather than hoping for the best without doing anything.

✖ *What you should not do:*

Fear conflict, so never speak out or do anything differently. Live in denial (pretend things are all right when they aren't). Follow self-destructive patterns and refuse to change.

Number 6:

✓ *What you should do:*

Learn that no one is perfect, nor are we meant to be. Learn and practise self-forgiveness and self-love. Develop a healthy self-esteem. Show compassion. Love without conditions. Be a 'people person' and use your natural wisdom to help others.

✗ *What you should not do:*

Lack self-esteem. Pretend to be someone else in order to please others. Judge yourself or others. Refuse to forgive yourself or others.

Number 7:

✓ *What you should do:*

Be willing to learn and always have an open mind. Be patient. Be intuitive. Trust yourself. Learn from experience and pass on to others what you learn.

✖ *What you should not do:*

Be rigid in your beliefs. Be religious without showing compassion or unconditional love. Be impatient. Be distrustful. Never learn from the past.

Number 8:

✓ *What you should do:*

Have a happy balance between spiritual and physical needs. Physical needs include money, sexual satisfaction, shelter, food, good health and affection. Spiritual needs involve doing worthwhile things with your life, and making the world a better place by being here.

✖ *What you should not do:*

Place too much importance on material things and/or sexual satisfaction. Work only for money or social status. See the physical body only in relationships.

Number 9:

✓ *What you should do:*

Communicate about important things. Communicate with your spirit through meditation and dreams. Care about people, the planet and animals. Be observant. Let go of things you no longer need.

✗ *What you should not do:*

Be too shy to communicate, or believe that no one will listen to you. Hoard things from the past and refuse to admit when things have come to a natural end. Refuse to connect with others or to understand them.

Number 11:

✓ *What you should do:*

Fulfil your vision. Imagine the future and bring it into reality. Communicate with angels and spirit guides. See the 'divine perfection' in others and remember that it's what the person can be, rather than what they actually are.

What you should not do:

Forget to be human. Dream your life away. Be over-idealistic and too easily disappointed. Look up to people. Fear death or fear spirits.

2: What Your Life Path Means

Now you know what your Life Path Number is, how does it apply to your life? As you have read, each number has a meaning. When we are doing what we're meant to be doing, we are going to succeed. When we are unaware of what our destiny is, or unwilling to follow it, then we are more likely to fail. It's that simple! If you realise you haven't been fulfilling your life path, now is the time to change.

Use the Guide to What Numbers Mean above as a basic tool from which to work. As you get to know their meanings you will be able to see more clearly the path you are meant to take. Look at your own Life Path Number. Are you doing what you should be doing? You'll know if you are, because you'll feel happy and successful. If you don't feel this way, ask yourself what you need to do differently to bring about a different result.

Now let's take a look at some famous people. See for yourself if they are fulfilling their life path. Note: as you will see from below, it's important to get into the habit of writing down the numbers in the way shown. My motto for this chapter is: 'Start as you mean to go on!'

A Number 1 Life Path

Irish Taoiseach and leader of Fianna Fáil, Bertie Ahern, was born on the 12th of September 1951.

```
12   09   19   51
 3    9    1    6
    3         7
         1
```

That gives Bertie a Number 1 Life Path, the perfect number for a leader and a decision maker.

Prince Harry of the British Royal Family was born on the 15th of September 1984. Note on this example that the last two digits in the year Harry was born – 8 and 4 – add up to a two digit number. Work out for yourself how this becomes Number 3 at the end of the second line on the following page.

```
15   09   19   84
 6    9    1    3
    6         4
         1
```

Despite being the second-born, it is very likely Harry may become king, rather than his brother, William, as he is following a Number 1 Life Path.

A Number 2 Life Path
Actress Bridget Fonda (niece of Jane) was born on the 27th of January 1954.

$$27 \quad 01 \quad 19 \quad 54$$
$$9 \quad \ 1 \quad \ 1 \quad \ 9$$
$$1 \qquad \quad 1$$
$$2$$

Being a Number 2, perhaps she is destined to fulfil secondary roles, especially in relation to her more famous aunt.

A Number 3 Life Path
Singer Celine Dion was born on the 30th of March 1968.

$$30 \quad 03 \quad 19 \quad 68$$
$$3 \quad \ 3 \quad \ 1 \quad \ 5$$
$$6 \qquad \quad 6$$
$$12$$
$$3$$

So Celine's Life Path is 3, perfect for expressing both joy and heartache in her singing. Expression is vital to the Number 3 Life Path, and it seems Irish actor Pierce Brosnan is following his destiny too (birthday 16th of May 1953). Check out his Life Path Number yourself!

A Number 4 Life Path

The Number 4 is about someone who works hard to get to the top and refuses to be a slave. The American broadcaster Oprah Winfrey was born on the 29th of January 1954.

$$29 \quad 01 \quad 19 \quad 54$$
$$2 \quad\quad 1 \quad\quad 1 \quad\quad 9$$
$$3 \quad\quad\quad\quad\quad 1$$
$$4$$

Other hard-working success stories belong to President Mary McAleese (27th of June 1951) and former leader of the British Conservative party John Major (29th of March 1943).

A Number 5 Life Path

Singer Tina Turner's had to face a lot of conflict to become the success she is today. She had to break some bad patterns she had been repeating. It's no surprise that her Life Path Number is 5 (26th of November 1939).

26	11	19	39
8	2	1	3
1		4	
	5		

Tiger Woods, the world-class golfing champion, is another Number 5. By setting himself constructive goals, and following positive patterns, he has stayed at the top year after year. (Date of birth: 25th of December 1975.)

A Number 6 Life Path

The Number 6 is all about the need for self-esteem and what is known as unconditional love. American actor Christopher Reeve (who played Superman) had a horse-riding accident which left him paralysed. Instead of buckling under the disaster, he had enough esteem for himself to slowly heal. He is now a wonderful model for others in a similar state.

Sadly, when someone is unable to feel love and compassion towards themselves and others, over time they can become capable of terrible crimes against humanity. Timothy McVeigh, who was found guilty of planting the Oklahoma bomb which killed many children and adults, is one such example. He was born on the 23rd of April 1968.

```
23   04   19   68
 5    4    1    5
     9         6
         15
         6
```

A Number 7 Life Path

The actress Julia Roberts was born on the 28th of October 1967. See her numbers, as set out below:

```
28   10   19   67
 1    1    1    4
     2         5
         7
```

Her Life Path Number is 7. Singer Sinead O'Connor has the same number (date of birth: 8th of December 1967). Being a Number 7 certainly explains why she is constantly searching, and why religion is so important to her.

A Number 8 Life Path

Former Irish President Mary Robinson's birthday is the 21st of May 1944.

$$
\begin{array}{cccc}
21 & 05 & 19 & 44 \\
3 & 5 & 1 & 8 \\
8 & & 9 & \\
& 17 & & \\
& 8 & &
\end{array}
$$

Her Life Path Number is 8. This number is about doing things that make a difference. When she fulfilled her role as first woman president of Ireland, she then went on to the United Nations.

Many people who want to make a difference also have a Number 8 Life Path Number. Examples are Irish politicians Des O'Malley (2nd of February 1939) and Ruairi Quinn (2nd of April 1946), and broadcaster Pat Kenny (29th of January 1949). Often people who are very interested in material things have the same number. But they search for something that is missing in their lives until they find it. One example is film star Elizabeth Taylor (27th of February 1932) who found joy by helping people with AIDS.

A Number 9 Life Path

Communicating is very important to someone with a Number 9 Life Path. They are often in careers such as broadcasting, singing or performing. Singer/songwriter Robbie Williams is one such person (date of birth: 13th of February 1974), as is performer and novelist Pauline McLynn (11th of July 1962).

A Number 11 Life Path

As you know, for our purposes the number 10 is 1 + 0, which makes 1, so there is no Number 10 Life Path Number. Number 11 follows 9, and is the final number in the Life Path. Usually we would add 1+1 to make 2, but this is a special number so we leave it as it is. Former American President Bill Clinton has a Number 11 Life Path, and was born on the 19th of August 1946:

$$
\begin{array}{cccc}
19 & 08 & 19 & 46 \\
1 & 8 & 1 & 1 \\
9 & & 2 & \\
& 11 & &
\end{array}
$$

Irishwoman Adi Roche is also a Number 11. She started the Children of Chernobyl campaign. This gives these children a chance of a carefree, healthy holiday in Ireland. Number 11 people often 'go the extra mile'. As visionaries they can see what is possible, rather than consider only what is probable.

Here's a list of some other stars' birthdates. Choose your favourites and work out their Life Path Numbers for yourself.

David Beckham:	2nd May 1975
Ronnie Biggs:	9th August 1929
Garth Brooks:	7th February 1962
Karen Carpenter:	2nd March 1950
Cindy Crawford:	20th February 1966
Danny De Vito:	17th November 1944
Marion Finucane:	21st February 1950
Mel Gibson:	3rd January 1956
Whitney Houston:	9th August 1963
Martin Luther King:	15th January 1929
Bette Midler:	1st December 1945
Van Morrison:	31st September 1945
Daniel O'Donnell:	12th December 1961
Sonia O'Sullivan:	28th November 1969
Luciano Pavarotti:	12th October 1935
Cliff Richard:	14th October 1940
Frank Sinatra:	12th December 1915
Elizabeth Taylor:	27th February 1932
Ronan Tynan:	14th May 1960
Denzel Washington:	28th December 1954

Whose Life Path Number do you share? Can you see where you may be similiar in some ways? If you'd like to be more like that person, what changes should you make in your own life to have more success?

3: What Do We Need To Learn?

I believe we have all come to Earth to learn lessons, a bit like attending 'The University of Life'. Those lessons relate to developing ourselves and finding the meaning of our life. As I wrote above, we each have a destiny, and we're given the 'blueprint' or 'map' in the make-up of our date of birth.

How do we uncover the messages in the blueprint? Look at the way I set out the life paths above. You will see four lines of figures. The first line is the date of birth. The second line tells us what we need to learn from birth to around the age of 40. The third line tells us what we need to do after 40 years of age. The fourth line is the Life Path Number.

Take singer Tina Turner's numbers:

Line 1	26	11	19	39
Line 2	8	2	1	3
Line 3		1		4
Line 4			5	

Now refer to the Guide to What Numbers Mean. Tina Turner had to learn to break bad patterns so that she could become free and enjoy her talents. She had to face conflict and make changes in order to build the life that she wanted. It was not enough just to hope that things would change by themselves. That is what the Number 5 Life Path suggests.

How was she to do this? Look at each of the numbers on the second line: 8, 2, 1 and 3. This is a map to the problems and how to overcome them. Check in the Guide to What Numbers Mean what each of these numbers offers, both the easy lessons and the hard lessons. Often when people have a hard life they are going against what they should be doing. So Tina Turner was living in extremes (8). She was a victim of other people's abuse (2). She let other people make decisions for her (1). She never expressed how she felt (3).

Then she had some hard knocks and began to learn. Now look at the numbers on line three: 1 and 4. By the time Tina Turner was 40 years old, she had begun to stand up for herself, work alone and make her own decisions (1). She faced a lot of her fears and made herself stable and secure (4). Tina Turner has certainly turned her life around. She is now a woman who has built her own life (5) and goes from success to success.

Now let's take a look at Oprah Winfrey. Her destiny is to 'face the fear and do it anyway', and become self-empowered.

$$29 \quad 01 \quad 19 \quad 54$$
$$2 \quad 1 \quad 1 \quad 9$$
$$3 \qquad \quad 1$$
$$4$$

When a number is repeated in one line, this usually reveals the lesson which is the most difficult to learn. In her early years (line 2), Oprah has a number 2. What does this suggest? Look again at the Guide to What Numbers Mean. What you shouldn't do: be co-dependent. Blame others for what happens to you. Feel like a victim of life.

Oprah has said that she was abused as a child. That made her feel very lonely and isolated (two Number 1s). She felt no one would listen to her (Number 9). She could so easily have turned to drugs or drink to run away from what happened to her. But she didn't. Instead, she set herself a goal. She forced herself to stand up and be herself.

As a woman in broadcasting and an Afro-American, this was not easy. She spoke out and became popular by airing issues that concerned the viewers at large (9). She wanted to make the world a better place. As she went into her forties, Oprah expressed what had happened and how she felt (3). She then became one of the top chat show hosts in the world (1).

Through all those lessons she has certainly achieved her Life Path and, not only that, has helped others to do so, too.

Work out some of the stars' Life

Path Numbers (pages 30–31). Look at the make-up of their first 40 years, then the rest of their life. Can you see how they have used their talents to gain success, or repeated bad habits and so lost their way?

Now look at the make-up of your own Life Path Number. Look at both the second and the third lines. What have you had to learn? Have you faced those lessons yet? What have you to look forward to in the future? Take special notice of where a number is repeated. This is where the more difficult lessons can be found. Have you passed those 'tests' yet?

4: The Inner Need Number

One of the most important things we need to discover is what makes us do the things we do. If we don't understand this, we won't understand why we act as we do. This can lead to a life lived in fear, and that's no life.

Don't panic! We can discover our motives for doing what we do by working out our Inner Need Number. We do this by looking at the vowels in our full name. The vowels are the letters A, E, I, O and U. Each vowel is given a number, and when we add up the numbers, the final figure is the Inner Need Number.

It's important to know that if you were given the name Margaret, but call yourself Maggie, you should use the name Maggie to work out your Inner Need Number. Or if your name is Peter James, but you call yourself PJ, then PJ is the name you should now use. And if you've changed your surname, your new surname is the one that is required.

Below are the numbers for the vowels:

A E I O U
1 5 9 6 3

Just to show a few examples, let's look at the Inner Need Number of Julia Roberts. We start by writing out her name. Then we put the numbers under the vowels, like so:

J U L I A R O B E R T S
3 9 1 6 5

Now we add up those vowels:

$$3 + 9 + 1 + 6 + 5 = 24$$
$$2 + 4 = 6$$

Julia's Inner Need Number is 6. It's no wonder she seeks her self-esteem through other people's eyes, on the cinema screen.

Another person who needs to put himself in the spotlight to gain self-esteem is Pat Kenny.

P AT K E N N Y

1   5

Adding up those two figures gives him a Number 6 Inner Need. Even if he called himself Patrick Kenny, he would still have the same Inner Need Number. See for yourself.

Let's look at Oprah Winfrey's vowels:

O P R A H W I N F R E Y

6   1   9   5

Now add the numbers:

$$6 + 1 + 9 + 5 = 21$$
$$2 + 1 = 3$$

As we know, 3 is the number of expression!

You can see how easy it is to find out what makes someone tick just by knowing their name. Just as in the Life Path, problems can arise when a number is repeated. The lesson in life is set out in the meaning of the repeated number. Take Bill Clinton as an example. He was given the name William Clinton, so let's look at his Inner Need Number with those vowels:

W I L L I A M C L I N T O N
9   9 1   9   6
$$9 + 9 + 1 + 9 + 6 = 34$$

Adding 3 = 4 gives us an Inner Need Number of 7. This number is about trust and learning lessons. Because he has three 9s he may have felt no one listened to him and a great need for secrecy arose because of this. However, as 'Bill' Clinton, rather than 'William', he gets rid of one of those extra 9s but also the number 1, which is about standing alone.

$$\begin{array}{c} \text{B I L L C L I N T O N} \\ 9 \qquad\quad 9 \qquad 6 \end{array}$$

As Bill Clinton, his Inner Need is:

$$9 + 9 + 6 = 24$$
$$2 + 4 = 6$$

This shows a need for love and a need to seek self-esteem through other people's eyes. Now that his term of presidency has ended he will need to find some way to stay in the limelight.

Sinead O'Connor also has a number repeated. Look at the vowels in her name:

SINEADOCONNOR

9 5 1 6   6   6

Add up those numbers and you get a total of 33. This makes an Inner Need Number 6. So Sinead, too, is seeking love and self-esteem, but she may be looking for it in the wrong places. The fact that the number 6 is repeated 3 times in the make-up of her name reflects that.

You can take some of your favourite stars and see how they are fulfilling their Inner Need. Remember to use only the vowels in their name. Note any number that is repeated. What does that tell you about the person? Now compare the Inner Need Number with the Life Path Number. Are any numbers repeated? What would that suggest to you?

What's your Inner Need?
Write out your name and place the numbers under each of the vowels.

Put your Inner Need Number in a circle.

For example:

This symbolises how you fulfil yourself by filling this void. Look at the numbers and see if you are fulfilling yourself positively, as shown on the Guide to What Numbers Mean. Do you need to change something in your life? What might you be repeating?

If you're called something such as P J Flynn you'll notice there are no vowels. In that case you may discover you never look after your own needs, that you're always at someone else's beck and call. Time to change your name, or the spelling if you want to change your life!

5: The Year You Are In

We live in cycles of nine years. It's as if we are given a garden to plant, tend and harvest over this timespan. Then when that garden has died, we are given a new garden so we begin afresh.

During each of those nine years there is a special job for you to do. Once we know what we're meant to be doing, that's the first step on the road to success.

The year you are in at present is known as your Personal Year. The important thing to know is that your Personal Year begins on the day of your birthday each year. So, unless you were born on the 1st of January, this is not the start of your new year.

As I wrote earlier, usually we fail because we are doing something at the wrong time. When we know exactly when we are meant to begin or finish something, then we are more likely to be a great success. It's what's known as working smart, not hard, and I am a great believer in it!

The way to find out your Personal Year is very simple. You just write out the full date of your last birthday, then add up the numbers. The final digit is your Personal Year.

My birthday is on the 17th of February. The last birthday I had was on the 17th of February 2001.

$$17 \quad 02 \quad 20 \quad 01$$
$$8 \quad\; 2 \quad\; 2 \quad\; 1$$
$$1 \qquad\quad 3$$
$$4$$

So, at the time of writing this (summer 2001) I am in a Number 4 Personal Year. As you see below, I put it in a symbol that looks like an arrowhead pointing upwards. That shows I've got my two feet on earth but am looking upwards for help.

Write out the date of your last birthday. Make sure you get the year right. Put your number into the special Personal Year symbol, as below:

When you get used to using these symbols for Life Path Number, Inner Need Number and Personal Year, you will be able to tell at a glance where you're going and what you should be doing.

Now check out on the following

pages what each Personal Year has to offer.

The way to understand the 9-year cycle is to imagine it as looking after a garden. During the first year there's nothing sown, but the more you look after it the better it will be as the cycle comes to a natural end over the following eight years.

A Number 1 Year:

This is the first year of a new 9-year cycle. You have a chance to start something new this year. Or you could begin again on an old project if it didn't take off before. Try to imagine your life as being like a garden. You want the things you work at to bloom and bring you a great harvest. So it helps to know that your actions in this Number 1 Year sow the seeds for the following eight years in this cycle.

Find out who you are this year. What are you meant to be doing in this life? If you start a new job or a new project this year you should find it easier to get into the swing of things. You'll find things just fall into place because this is the right time for new beginnings, so enjoy it!

✓ *A Number 1 Year is about:*

Getting to know yourself
New beginnings
Doing something different
A new approach to an old problem

✗ *So avoid:*

Being lonely
Feeling cut off
Repeating old patterns

A Number 2 Year:

This is the second year of the current cycle. In a Number 2 year you are tending the garden you have sown in your previous year. You want your garden to blossom and bring you a great harvest. A newly sown plant needs care, and a Number 2 Year is for working with people and things, and being part of a team. It's also a year for making decisions. This year you can respond in a new way to get a new outcome!

A Number 2 Year is a good year for spending time with someone you love and building up a very strong relationship. In a family, make sure you show that you are part of their team, take time for other members, and realise that it's quality, not quantity, that counts in the end.

✓ *A Number 2 Year is about:*

Looking after what you began last year
Working with others
Making decisions
One-to-one relationships

✗ *So avoid:*

Acting like a victim
Being too needy
Refusing to make decisions

A Number 3 Year:

In a Number 3 Year you must show your emotions and be creative. Watch the words you use. If you say or think, 'I'll never get that job', or, 'I never have enough money', that's what's likely to happen! Change your mind this year and imagine being happy and wealthy. Soon you'll find that that positive image becomes real in your life. It has certainly worked for me!

Be creative, be open about your

feelings. Start a diary, paint a picture, or paint the bathroom! Sing in the shower, dig the garden, dance in the dark. No one has to know what you're doing. Then you'll be creating a happy and healthy life. One other very important thing you can create this year is a baby!

A Number 3 Year is about:

Fun and laughter
Being creative
Showing how you feel
Using positive thoughts and words

So avoid:

Holding back on how you feel
Being sad
Negative thoughts and words

A Number 4 Year:

A Number 4 Year is about hard work that helps you to become safe and secure in the long term. This year it's important to focus on what you want. If you don't you might be working all the time, just like a slave. So set a goal and work towards it. This might mean you have to 'weed out' some things you started in your first year. This is so that the more important things can grow.

In a Number 4 Year you need to 'feel the fear and do it anyway', and so break through any barriers holding you back.

✓ *A Number 4 Year is about:*

Setting goals

Hard work

Facing fears

Breaking through barriers

✗ *So avoid:*

Being a slave

Letting fear hold you back

Lacking focus

A Number 5 Year:

In a Number 5 Year you are more than

halfway through your 9-year cycle. If you've worked hard so far you'll now begin to see results – just as buds begin to show in your garden before they come into full bloom. A Number 5 Year gives you the chance to face conflict and bring about change. Often we hide from conflict and pretend things are okay when they are not.

This is the year to kick a bad habit. Even more weeding may be needed. If you smoke or drink too much, put up with bad behaviour, or repeat mistakes, you'll find it's easier to stop this year. So give it a go! Try to build a happy, healthy life just as you would take care in building a great house or a beautiful garden.

A Number 5 Year is about:

Making changes

Facing conflict

Starting new patterns of behaviour

Building a new lifestyle

✖ *So avoid:*

Hiding from conflict
Living in denial
Repeating bad behaviour patterns

A Number 6 Year:

This year is about love and self-esteem. It's vital to love yourself before you can accept true love from someone else. Self-esteem is how you see your own worth. Do you feel you're worthwhile? Do you deserve good things in your life? In this year you may feel you deserve better than your present life and love. If so, do not settle for second best.

None of us are meant to be perfect. We can only do our best. Learn to laugh at yourself, and at life. Then you can love yourself, and truly love others.

✔ *A Number 6 Year is about:*

Having a healthy self-esteem

Loving yourself and others
Romance

 So avoid:

Judging yourself
Low self-esteem
Judging others

A Number 7 Year:

A Number 7 Year is all about learning and being patient. There's so much to learn it seems like there's no end to it! You may like to study for exams this year, or attend a course or workshop to learn about something new.

This is a good time to seek other people's opinions, but make your choice based on your own instinct. Instinct is another word for 'intuition'. This means 'tuition' that you get from 'inside yourself'. When you follow your intuition you can be sure you're on the right road.

✓ *A Number 7 Year is about:*

Trusting your inner voice
Learning
Being patient

✗ *So avoid:*

Putting more trust in others than in yourself
Being impatient
Repeating mistakes

A Number 8 Year:

A Number 8 Year means it's harvest time! You've worked hard, you've planned things out, you've been patient and now you are going to reap your rewards. This is the year when you can bring in that plentiful harvest. All the work you have put into your present cycle will now pay you back. Open your arms to receive your rewards!

This is also a good year for buying or selling property, or investing your money. Balance is important, so don't go overboard. It's also a year when you may find you need more out of life than just money, so do something that makes a difference. The Number 8 looks like two rings joined together, so it could be a good year for marriage.

✓ *A Number 8 Year is about:*

Enjoying your harvest
Doing things that matter
Being balanced in your life

✗ *So avoid:*

Going overboard
Wasting money

A Number 9 Year:

This is the last year of your present cycle. Just as in nature, you'll find that in a Number 9 Year, lots of things come to a natural end. Look at a garden at the end of the year: everything seems to have died off and there's no new growth around. The garden isn't dead, it's just resting. Your life is like the garden. You've done a good job and now it's time to take a break and rest. Only by doing this can you begin afresh in your next 9-year cycle.

This is the year to finish things. Make an extra effort to clear the desk, to clean the house, to finish off that project. Everything will work towards you finishing things this year, so try not to start anything that you want to last for a long time.

✓ *A Number 9 Year is about:*

Finishing things off
Doing things left on the 'long finger'
Clearing out old things

✗ *So avoid:*

Starting a long-term project
Seeking a long-term romance
Holding on to old hurts

YOUR SEASONS

Just like in nature, your Personal Year is divided into four seasons: spring, summer, autumn and winter. By working within each season you can make sure you're doing the right thing at the right time! As your year begins on the day of your birthday, that is the first day of your springtime. Each season lasts for three months.

Take my birthday: 17th February. The 17th of February is the first day of my spring, and this lasts until the 16th of May.

Spring

Spring is the time for starting off new projects, for 'planting seeds'. Whatever I do in my springtime I know I will be reaping the benefit of it later in my year. I need to be patient and realise that it's not possible to enjoy my harvest just yet.

Summer

Spring is followed by summer, which in my case starts on the 17th of May and goes on until the 16th of August each year. The summer is a very busy time. Everything I have sown is now beginning to grow. I might decide to weed out a few things that aren't doing so well. Then I can tend better to the projects I want to blossom.

Autumn

In my case, this season begins on the 17th of August and lasts for the next three months until the 16th of November. The autumn is the time to harvest all the things I worked on during my spring and summer months. If I've been patient then I'm going to benefit a lot. This is possibly my favourite time of my year.

Winter

If my autumn has paid me back for all the hard work I put in during the year, then my winter can be a time to sit back and relax and live off my winter store. Some things will die down naturally, just like the last leaves fall off the trees during this season. It doesn't mean the trees are dead, just that they are taking a break so that they can store up energy for the next burst of activity the following spring.

My winter season is from the 17th of November until the 16th of February. Usually I spend this time relaxing and reflecting on what I did in the past year, and planning what I want to do in the following one. The secret is to plan ahead but don't plant just yet. Very little will grow in the winter and you can be very disappointed if you waste a lot of energy.

For many years I started new things on January 1st, not knowing I was in my winter season. It's no wonder they didn't take off!

Now work out your seasons, beginning on your birthday with your three months of spring. If you look back you may find, like me, that you were doing things at the wrong time.

Also take a look back at your recent Personal Year cycle. Do you know now why certain things happened during those years? Now you know what to do within each Personal Year, and the right season to work in. From today you can work smart, not hard!

You now have three vital keys to your life:

- Your **Life Path Number** says what you should be doing in your life.
- Your **Inner Need Number** shows what motivates you.

●Your **Personal Year** shows when you should be doing certain things and the personal season in which to do them.

If you put the symbol for your Life Path

over the symbols for your Inner Need

and Personal Year

notice what sign you make.

It's very much like the sign of the Star of David, which is a very old symbol. In fact, it is believed that the science of numbers was first found by the seers of the Hebrews. They were slaves in Egypt about 7,000 years ago.

6: Some Interesting Numbers

Numbers don't just have importance for people. Countries have their own numbers, as do world events. Just look at these.

You can discover the numbers of a country, and see how they change as the dates of legal agreements are put in place. Ireland is a good example.

The Constitution of Ireland was agreed in a referendum on the 1st of July 1937 (which adds up to a Number 1, suggesting the start of something new). Then the Republic of Ireland Act was passed on the 21st of December

1948 (adding up to another Number 1). But it wasn't put into action until the 18th of April 1949, which gives the Republic of Ireland the Life Path Number 9.

$$18 \quad 04 \quad 19 \quad 49$$

$$9 \quad 4 \quad 1 \quad 4$$

$$4 \quad\quad 5$$

$$9$$

Looking at the make-up of numbers on the second line you can see that the number 4 appears twice. When this number is repeated, what does it mean? (See 'What you should not do' in the Guide to What Numbers Mean.) It is not until we break this bad pattern that we become self-empowered (Number 4) and free (Number 5). Then we can fulfil our Life Path, Number 9, which is about communication, helping others, and letting go of the past.

We can call this country two different names. Add up the following Inner Need Numbers – the vowels:

R E P U B L I C O F I R E L A N D

5　3　　9　6　9　5　　1

The Inner Need is Number 11. This number is about having vision and being dream-like. Of course we need to be realistic too!

By just calling it Ireland, we get a different Inner Need:

I R E L A N D

9　5　　1

The Inner Need Number is 6. Now you know why there are so many successful media people from Ireland. It's because people from Ireland are so popular! It's also a country where compassion and love needs to be shown instead of judgement.

Let's have a look at some other countries.

The American Declaration of Independence from Britain happened on the 4th of July 1776.

$$04 \quad 07 \quad 17 \quad 76$$

$$4 \quad 7 \quad 8 \quad 4$$

$$2 \qquad 3$$

$$5$$

As you can see, it adds up to a Life Path Number 5. This can often mean change through conflict, especially as there are two of the Number 4 in the make-up of the second line. The American War of Independence lasted from 1775 to 1783. France also joined the country to fight against Britain, so there was lots of conflict.

Later, after their Civil War (1861–
1865), America became the United
States of America. If you look at the
vowels of this name, you will find they
add up to an Inner Need Number of 9:

UNITEDSTATESOFAMERICA

3　9　5　　　1　5　6　1　5　9　1

　　　　　　　　　　　= 45

4 + 5 = 9

The USA certainly likes to have its
voice heard and it welcomes a lot of
strangers to its shores.

However, when you look at the
smaller name, USA, you will see a
different number for its Inner Need:

U S A

3 + 1 = 4

Or do you prefer to say 'The States'?
This adds up to an Inner Need
Number 11. This is the same as

Ireland's Inner Need Number. It's no wonder people from the Republic of Ireland get on so well in The States!

Ireland, England, Denmark, France, Germany, Israel. Such differing countries, yet they all share the same Inner Need Number. Check it out for yourself. Now look at the Inner Need Number of the United Kingdom, Great Britain, Britain and the UK. It's possible you react differently depending on which term is used because they have different Inner Need Numbers.

Numbers show us so many things. The sinking of the ship the Lusitania, which was one of the reasons the USA entered the First World War, happened on the 7th of May 1915. Add up those numbers and you get the Number 1. So that was a day which began some very important world changes. The

Second World War began on the 1st of September 1939, which adds up to a Number 5, another day of conflict! On the 13th of October 1943 (a Number 4 day) Italy declared war on its former ally, Germany, which certainly helped in the long run to bring that war to an end. And more recently, the 11th of September 2001 proved to be a day of huge conflict in the world (it adds up to Number 5).

Another powerful day (Number 4) was the 1st of January 1973, when Britain, Ireland and Denmark became members of the Common Market. After a lot of hard work the Common Market finally grew into the European Union.

It is interesting to see how many 'firsts' there have been on a date that adds up to the Number 1. James Ross discovered the North Magnetic Pole on the 15th of April 1800. In 1808 on the 1st of January, the US Congress banned importation of slaves. On the 1st of January 1961, the birth control pill was introduced to the UK. On the 29th of June 1964, the US Civil Rights Act was passed. On the very same day, the pilot of the popular TV series *Star Trek*, then called *The Cage*, was released.

SOME INTERESTING LIVES

Look at the Life Path Number and Inner Need Number of the following people who lived rather short lives:

Marilyn Monroe, born Norma Jean Mortenson (also known as Baker), on 1st June 1926. Died 4th August 1962.

Janis Joplin, born 19th January 1943. Died 4th January 1970.

Marc Bolan, born Mark Feld, on 30th September 1947. Died 16th September 1977.

Princess Diana (also known as Di), born Lady Diana Spencer on 1st July 1961. Died 31st August 1997.

CONCLUSION

I hope you have enjoyed reading this book and learning more about yourself and others through numbers. Numbers are fun and, as I wrote at the start, you don't have to be a whizz at maths to learn from them. But when you get used to them, you'll find that it all adds up!